Eyewitness

Stories of the power of Jesus

Gordon Jaquiery

About the Author

Gordon Jaquiery has always been a storyteller, whether as a schoolteacher, a Bible teacher, a builder, a gardener or a sports fan.

These stories were first read aloud to children's church as a way of presenting the timeless importance of stories in the Bible. This is the first time he has put his stories into print to share his inspiring and quirky viewpoint.

He lives by the beach in Titahi Bay, Wellington. He has three children and 16 grandchildren.

Eyewitness: Stories of the power of Jesus
© 2017 Gordon Jaquiery

ISBN 978-0-473-39216-1

Published by: Acumen
19 Trevor Terrace, Newtown
Wellington 6021, New Zealand

To order copies: *www.acumen.net.nz/pages/AcumenBooks.html* and leading online stores.
To contact the author: *eyewitness@acumen.net.nz*

All images and illustrations by Sara Lauridsen and from www.istockphoto.com

Disclaimer:
These stories come from the author's imagination based on Scripture but contain fictional characters.

Acknowledgments:
Thank you to the children of Titahi Bay Community Church for listening so well, you could hear a pin drop.

Special thanks to Mike Steer for being the driving force and encourager in the journey to take these stories from spoken to written word.

Also by Gordon Jaquiery:
Eyewitness: Stories before Jesus
Eyewitness: Stories from the life of Jesus
Eyewitness: Stories of Advent and Easter

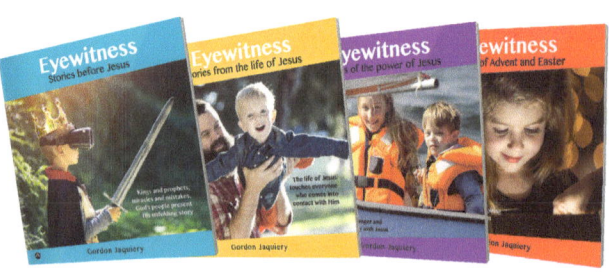

Contents

A meal to remember *(John 12 & 13)*	2
Remarkable events at Skull Hill *(John 19 & 20)*	4
A very special promise *(Acts 1 & Luke 24)*	6
Sensation in Jerusalem *(Acts 2)*	8
The death of a brave son *(Acts 6 & 7)*	10
A life changing journey *(Acts 8)*	12
An unlikely convert *(Acts 9)*	14
The good news is for everyone *(Acts 10)*	16
A prayer time to remember *(Acts 12)*	18
Not your normal prisoners *(Acts 16)*	20
A meeting of minds at Mars Hill *(Acts 17)*	22
The town clerk's story *(Acts 19)*	24
Trouble in Jerusalem *(Acts 24)*	26
Two Governors, a King and Paul *(Acts 25 & 26)*	28
Paul's dangerous voyage to Rome *(Acts 27 & 28)*	30
The man who nearly died *(Philippians 2: 25-30)*	32
A very special letter *(1 & 2 Timothy)*	34

A meal to remember

My name is **Philip** and I'm a disciple of Jesus. I want to tell you about some things that happened a few days before Jesus died.

We were in Jerusalem to celebrate the Passover festival. It's a very important feast for us because it reminds us of the time long ago when our people were slaves in Egypt. Jewish people like to celebrate Passover in Jerusalem at least once in their lives, so the city is always packed with visitors at this time.

Well, I was standing on a busy street looking at the crowds when some Greek people came up to me and said, "We are looking for a man called Jesus."

I wasn't sure what to say because Jesus usually only helps fellow Jews, so I asked Andrew what he thought and he said, "Let's take them to Jesus."

When we found Jesus he said a strange thing: "When you put a seed in the ground it remains just one seed unless it dies. Then you get lots of new seeds growing from it." And then he began to talk about how he was going to die.

It puzzled me at the time and I think it puzzled the Greek visitors too. But we had the Passover feast coming up that evening so my mind went to other things.

We had got the meal ready for our feast and we were sharing it together, all 12 of us disciples and Jesus, when there was a bit of an argument. Two people were boasting that they were the most important. It was quite embarrassing really, but suddenly Jesus stood up and we all went quiet.

What he did next shocked us. He took off his clothes and stood there in his underwear. He got a bucket, a cloth and some soap and he got down on his knees and began to wash our feet.

Now, in this part of the world we wear sandals because of the heat and there's a lot of pollution on the streets with animal droppings and so on, so washing people's feet is not a very nice job. It's what the servants do. We felt even more embarrassed because Jesus is our leader and he was doing the servant's job.

When Jesus got to Peter, Peter pulled his feet away from Jesus. He said, "Over my dead body, Jesus. You're not washing my feet." But Jesus explained to him that if he wanted to be part of God's kingdom he needed to let Jesus wash his feet. So Peter changed his tune. We were all pretty quiet after that, especially when Jesus said he was setting us an example to follow.

We were getting to the end of the meal when we noticed Jesus had become quite sad. He said, "One of you is going to hand me over to the people who want to kill me." Now that really shocked us, and Peter whispered to John (who was sitting next to Jesus), "Ask him who he's talking about." So John asked Jesus quietly and Jesus replied, "I'm going to give a piece of bread to the person I'm talking about." And he dipped a crust in the dish and handed it to Judas. Next thing, Judas got up and went out into the night.

I'll tell you what happened at the garden another time. It was incredibly sad. I have thought a lot about what Jesus said about a seed when the Greeks came to us. I think Jesus was telling us that he had to die so that anyone who believes in him could have this new life he

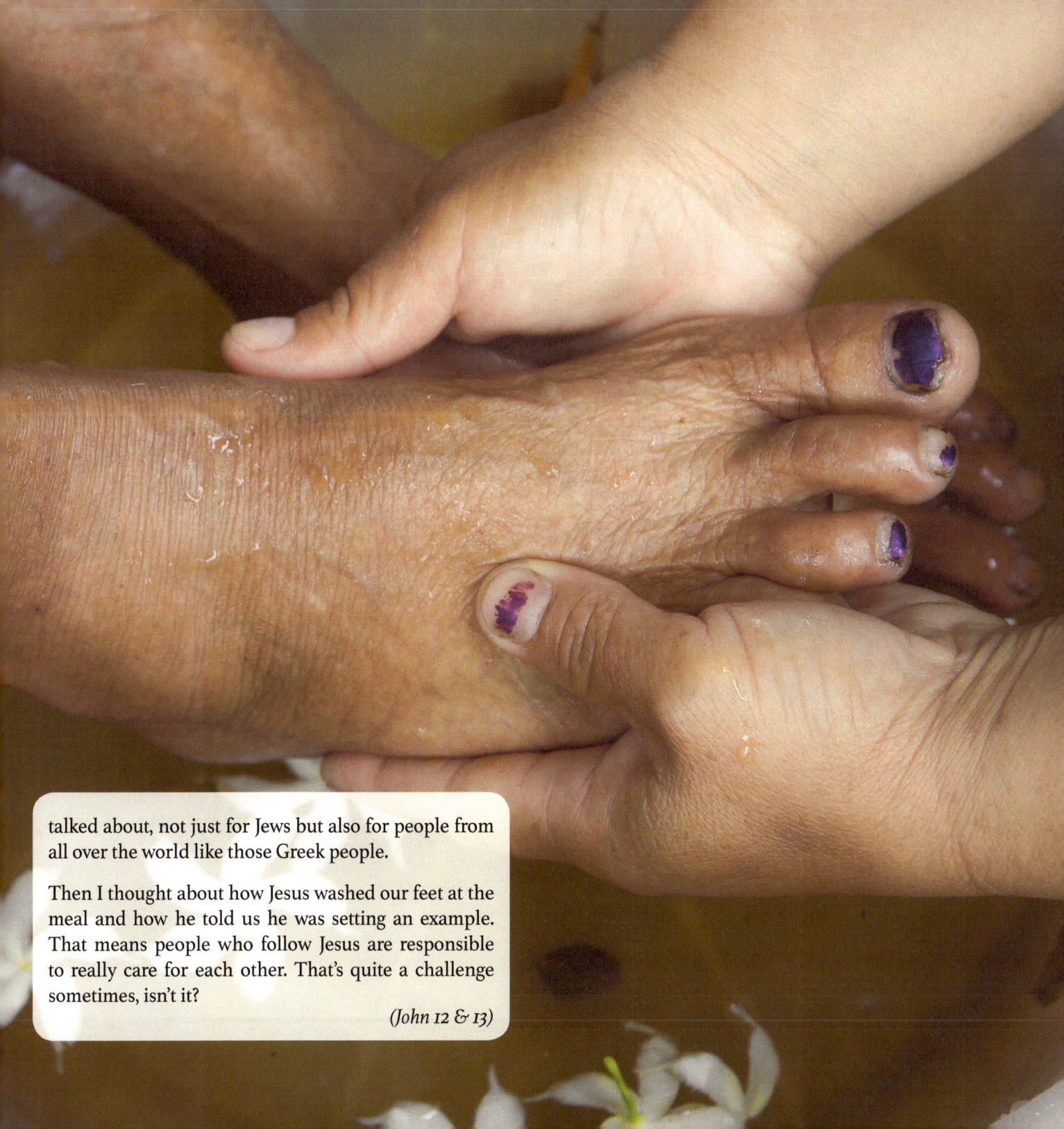

talked about, not just for Jews but also for people from all over the world like those Greek people.

Then I thought about how Jesus washed our feet at the meal and how he told us he was setting an example. That means people who follow Jesus are responsible to really care for each other. That's quite a challenge sometimes, isn't it?

(John 12 & 13)

Remarkable events at Skull Hill

It's **Philip** here again. Last time I told you the story of our last meal with Jesus. This time, I want to finish the story – and what an amazing ending it is.

It was quite dark when we arrived in the garden after finishing our Passover meal. We actually needed a flaming torch to see the path. Everyone was very tired by this time so when Jesus asked us to pray while He went away by himself for a bit, we couldn't keep our eyes open.

The next thing I remember was Jesus waking us up and a sudden, big commotion with lots of yelling and the glare of torch lights. And there was Judas, who had left the meal table early, with the people who hated Jesus. He was pointing at us. Some soldiers then grabbed Jesus, tied him up and took him off to the high priest.

At this point I was really scared. We all thought that Jesus would be the next leader of our country and here he was being treated like a criminal. I feel ashamed about it now, but in that moment I ran for my life and hid in a friend's home. I thought that if I kept out of sight for a few days I could save my own skin. Actually most of us disciples made a run for it, but John and Peter had a bit more courage than the rest of us and they followed the soldiers to the palace of the high priest.

John told me later what happened with the High Priest.

The priests decided that Jesus should be put to death because He said He was the Son of God, but only the Roman governor could order someone to be put to death. So in the morning they took Jesus to the governor – a man called Pilate.

There was a bit of a trial. The governor thought Jesus was innocent but he could see the Jews might start a riot if he let him go free. So in the end he gave in and Roman soldiers took Jesus out of the city to a place called Skull Hill - it's called that because the rock formation there looks like a human skull. There they put Jesus to death by nailing him to a cross, and they also executed two criminals at the same time. John saw it all from where he stood near the cross. Before he died, Jesus asked John to look after his mother.

What happened next was really spooky. It was the middle of the day and suddenly the whole country was clothed in darkness. It was no ordinary darkness – it was a thick clammy darkness that lasted three hours. I don't remember anything like it happening before.

As the darkness was starting to lift, at 3 o'clock in the afternoon, Jesus shouted out the word "Finished", and a short time later he died. Even the Roman soldier in charge of the executions was amazed and said that Jesus must have been the Son of God.

Soon after Jesus died, two of his secret followers, men called Joseph and Nicodemus, who had some influence with the governor, got permission to take the body of Jesus off the cross and bury him in a tomb owned by one of the men. It was a shallow cave carved out of the rocky hill not far from where Jesus died.

By this time it was evening and because the next day was our Sabbath we couldn't do any work. I remember just sitting there, staring into space and puzzling over all that had happened.

Then early on Sunday morning we had the most amazing news. A few of us were talking about what had

happened when along the road came some women who were also followers of Jesus. They were running. I'd never seen anything like it. People don't run in public unless they are criminals.

We called out, "What's going on?" They yelled at us, "Someone's stolen the body of Jesus. The tomb's empty except for his clothes." With that, Peter and John raced off to the tomb to see for themselves. When they came back they confirmed what the women had said.

We got together that night. There were 10 of us - Judas wasn't there of course, and no one knew where Thomas had gone. We had bolted the door in case the enemies of Jesus found us.

Suddenly, out of nowhere, Jesus was in the room with us. We couldn't believe this was real. Jesus was alive, talking to us and showing us the injuries to his body.

What a weekend we'd had. We were happy beyond words to see him. A lot more has happened since then, which I can tell you about some other time. The important thing to remember is this: Jesus really did come back from the dead.

(John 19 & 20)

A very special promise

My name is **Thomas** and I am one of the followers of Jesus. Actually, you may already know me. I was the guy who was so sad after Jesus was put to death that I left the disciples for a while. I was not there when Peter and the other disciples saw Jesus alive and talked to Him. I couldn't bring myself to believe it when I heard. That all changed a few days later, when I saw Jesus myself and He showed me His scarred hands and side.

And it wasn't just us disciples who saw Jesus, others saw Him as well, not just once but many times. On one special occasion there was a big crowd – hundreds and hundreds of us - and Jesus joined in. You can imagine how special that was.

We also talked to Jesus about what was going to happen next. We were all hoping that he would use his power to get rid of the Romans from our country and set up his new kingdom in Jerusalem. We were looking forward to being in charge with him.

But Jesus kept saying to us, "You've got the wrong idea. My kingdom is not just for the Jews. It's for everyone who believes in me. You are all going to have a part to play, but it will be different from what you are thinking about now."

Well, this went on for nearly 6 weeks.

I shall never forget the last time we saw Jesus. It was just outside Jerusalem and we were walking and talking together. We walked around the mountain we call Olivet because of all the olive trees that grow there. We went past the garden where the soldiers had arrested Jesus - that brought back some memories, I can tell you - and we continued along the road to Jericho.

When we reached the village of Bethany where our friends Mary, Martha and Lazarus lived, Jesus stopped and said to us, " I am going to leave you now. I am going to return to my Father in Heaven. Don't forget He is your Father too. What I want you to do is go back to Jerusalem and wait there. You don't need to do anything. Stay in Jerusalem. Remember how I told you about God sending a special person to be with you when I'm no longer with you physically? Well, that's going to happen in a few days time."

Then He said to us "Bless you all" and Jesus was taken up into the clouds and we never saw Him again after that. We all just stood there looking up into the clouds. I don't know how long we were there. It was so hard to take it all in. We just felt like laughing and crying at the same time as we thought of all that had happened since Jesus came into our lives only three years earlier.

The next thing we saw was two angels who said to us, "Don't just stand there looking up at the clouds. Jesus will come back one day, but in the meantime, do what He said. Go back to Jerusalem and wait for what He promised you."

So that's what we did. We walked the four kilometres back to Jerusalem, having no real idea of what to expect. But when it happened a few days later, we were just flabbergasted. It was the most amazing thing you could imagine.

(Acts 1 & Luke 24)

Sensation in Jerusalem

My name is **Tobias**, but my friends call me Toby. I'm a teenager and I live with my parents in Alexandria, a big city in Egypt. I speak two languages, Egyptian and Hebrew. Our ancestors are Jewish, but our family has lived in Egypt for over a hundred years. My father always said that when we had enough money we would visit Jerusalem to see where our family came from.

Well, we went last year and I want to tell you about what happened while we were in Jerusalem.

We were staying in a hostel for travellers. There were people there from all sorts of countries, mostly people like us though, Jews, who were making the trip of a lifetime to see their ancestral homeland.

We visited the Temple and lots of places we had read about in our sacred books. Then, one morning, after breakfast, my Dad said, "Let's take a walk to the town centre", so we set off together, Mum, Dad and me. As we got near the town square we noticed quite a crowd gathering and lots of noise, so, being curious, we joined the throng.

It was quite strange because there were different groups of people listening to different speakers. But they were speaking in languages we didn't understand. Then we came to a group listening to a man speaking in Egyptian, so we stopped to listen.

He was obviously one of the local people - in fact he looked like a fisherman, but he spoke perfect Egyptian, so my Dad called out, "When did you learn our language?" He replied, "I didn't, but something amazing has just happened."

He was a disciple of someone called Jesus. Now, we'd heard people talking about Jesus a few times since we arrived in Jerusalem. He was from Galilee in the north of the country. The Romans had killed him and there were all sorts of rumours that he had come back to life.

The man who was speaking in our language told us he'd seen Jesus after he was killed. He and his friends were told by Jesus to stay in Jerusalem and God would send his Spirit to make them strong. That morning they were all together praying and suddenly a great wind had blown upon them and they saw flames resting on each other's heads.

The man continued, "We were so overwhelmed we started to praise God for sending us his Spirit and when I opened my mouth I was speaking a language I had never learned. So I went into the street like the rest of my friends and you people from Egypt must have recognised the language. These other groups of people are listening in other languages. All I can say is that God has done a miracle this morning."

Well, we didn't know what to make to make of it all, and some people in the crowd started to scoff and say, "You must be drunk." But it was only 9 o'clock in the morning and people don't usually get drunk so early in the day.

But then another strange thing happened. Another man, who also looked like a fisherman, got up to speak and everyone went quiet. I learned afterwards that his name was Peter, one of Jesus' trusted disciples. I wrote down what he said:

"A couple of months ago, Jesus visited this city to tell you about the Kingdom of God, but you rejected him as a fraud and asked the Romans to kill him. Well, you couldn't have been more wrong. You put the Messiah, the Son of God, to death and to show you how wrong you are, God has raised him from the dead. You people in Jerusalem have done an evil thing."

Well that really set the crowd off. Some started crying, some were shouting, some were tearing their clothes and saying, "What shall we do?" Then Peter said, "You need to be really sorry for what you have done and if you are, you will be forgiven and, to show you mean what you say, you can be baptised."

And that's what happened. Thousands of people asked to be baptised and my Dad said, "I believe this man Peter is telling the truth. Let's get baptised and be followers of Jesus." It was a really moving experience.

We are back in our home city of Alexandria now and we have started getting together with some other Christians. We always knew our visit to Jerusalem would be a special time, but it's turned out to be an absolutely life-changing experience for our family.

(Acts 2)

The death of a brave son

My name is **Tabitha** and I am a resident of Jerusalem. My story is a very sad one. Indeed, it's hard for me to talk about it without weeping, but I do want people to hear it. Let me begin by sharing a bit of the back story.

My family is Jewish and we have always attended our local synagogue regularly, but things changed recently. We are not welcome there anymore.

Our people have been hoping for many generations that God would send us a Saviour, a Messiah. Our sacred books, written hundreds of years ago, prophesied this would happen. Then Jesus of Nazareth came and some of us were drawn to Him. Everything seemed to point to Him being God's special person. However, our leaders in the Temple and the synagogues rejected Him and had Him put to death by the Romans.

Then we heard stories from His disciples that God had raised Him from the dead to show us He was the Son of God, the promised Messiah. Many people saw Him and I saw Him, too. There were hundreds of people present that day. It was an amazing experience and it removed any doubts that we had about Jesus.

A few weeks later, during the festival called Pentecost, God sent His Spirit to be with all those who had believed in Jesus. There were thousands of people who became Christians that day and my family were among them.

It was a wonderful time. Each day more and more people believed in Jesus, even some of the priests. We used to get together in people's homes to talk about our faith in Jesus and what was happening in our lives.

The Christian community was growing so fast in Jerusalem that the apostles decided we needed more leaders to guide us and I was so pleased when my son Stephen was chosen.

The apostles prayed for him and the other new leaders, and shortly after that God began to work some special miracles through Stephen. It was amazing and quite difficult for me as his mother to stay humble.

But then life began to get difficult for our new community. The people who had rejected Jesus as God's Son started to cause trouble for us. I think they were jealous of what they saw happening and they singled out my son Stephen as their target.

They made false accusations against him. They said he was speaking ill of Moses and the Temple, but Stephen was more than a match for them. He showed them from the sacred books of Moses and the Prophets that Jesus truly was God's promised Messiah. That only made his opponents more determined to destroy Stephen.

Then it all came to a head. That day will be in my memory forever. Stephen was brought before the High Priest and asked to answer the accusations against him. He showed them how past generations of Jewish leaders had often rejected God's messengers and told them that they were no different in refusing to believe in Jesus.

Well, that was the final straw for his accusers. They refused to listen to my son any longer. Some of them even covered their ears. They grabbed hold of Stephen, dragged him out of the city and threw stones at him till he died.

You can imagine how devastated I was to lose my son. My Christian friends supported me in my grief and

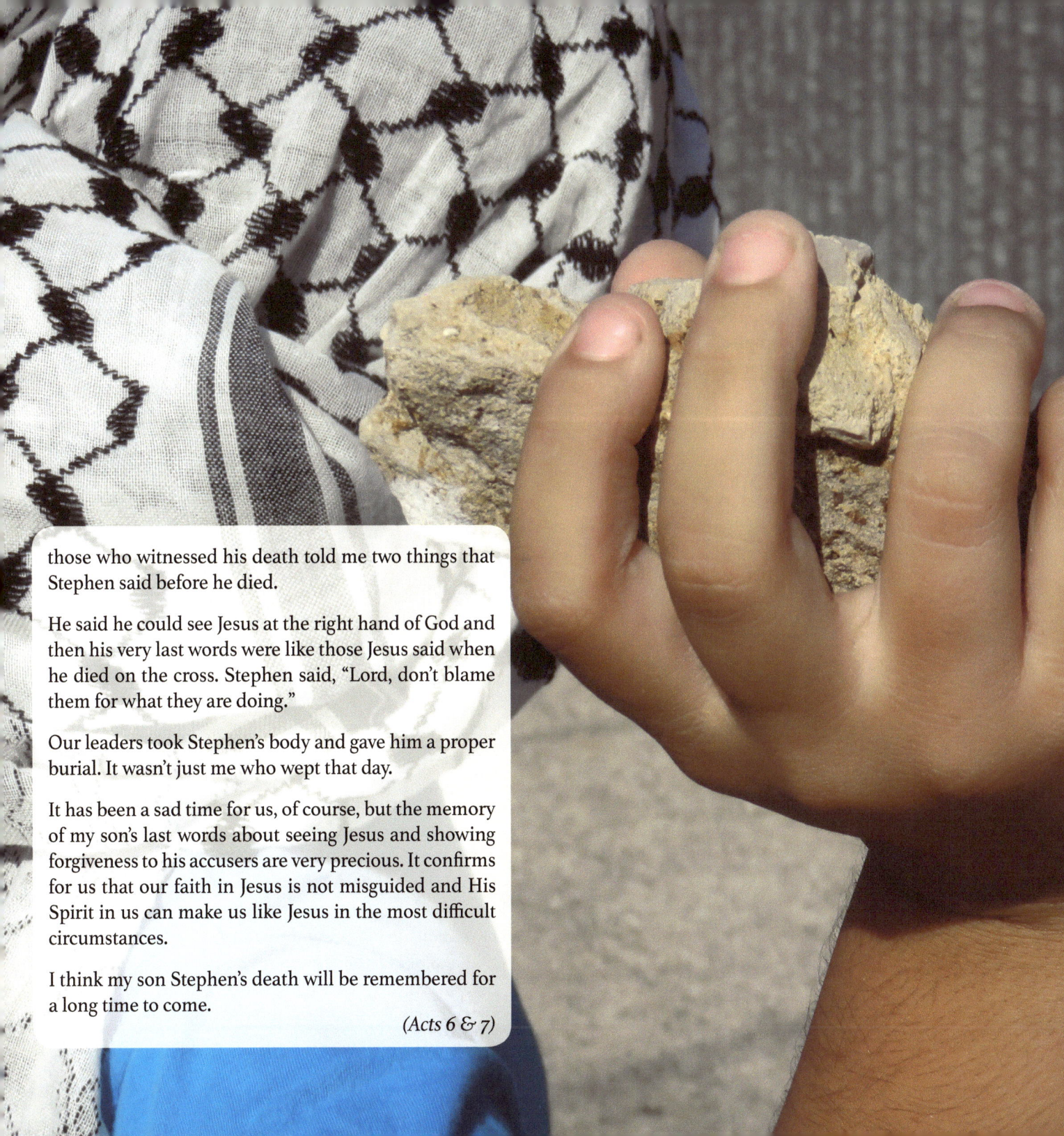

those who witnessed his death told me two things that Stephen said before he died.

He said he could see Jesus at the right hand of God and then his very last words were like those Jesus said when he died on the cross. Stephen said, "Lord, don't blame them for what they are doing."

Our leaders took Stephen's body and gave him a proper burial. It wasn't just me who wept that day.

It has been a sad time for us, of course, but the memory of my son's last words about seeing Jesus and showing forgiveness to his accusers are very precious. It confirms for us that our faith in Jesus is not misguided and His Spirit in us can make us like Jesus in the most difficult circumstances.

I think my son Stephen's death will be remembered for a long time to come.

(Acts 6 & 7)

A life changing journey

My name is **Ordu** and I live in Ethiopia where I am a civil servant in the government of our Queen Candace. I look after the country's finances and sometimes this requires me to travel. The story I want to tell you is about one journey that completely changed my life.

Perhaps I should begin with a bit of the background to what happened. Some of the people in this part of North Africa are descendants of refugees from the land of Israel. Their religion is different from mine. They believe there is only one God whom they call the "Lord".

I work with some of these people and I have been drawn to their beliefs, so when the opportunity arose to travel to their homeland of Israel I was quite excited.

Israel is a long way from Ethiopia, but I have my own transport and staff because of my high position in the government so the journey wasn't too difficult.

After I finished the government business I spent a few days in Jerusalem, visiting the places of interest in the city. I was also able to share in some of the worship at their great Temple, but not everything, because of my status as a foreigner.

Still, it was a good visit and just before I left Jerusalem I purchased a copy of one of the ancient Jewish writings. It was a Greek translation of the prophet Isaiah, written six hundred years ago. I thought it would be a good read on the long ride home.

We set off on the return journey and I settled into the chariot, made myself as comfortable as I was able, and took out my treasured scroll and started to read it.

However, the more I read, the more I became confused. Isaiah kept describing someone whom he called the "Servant" and I couldn't work out if he was talking about himself or some other person.

By this time, we were travelling through some rough terrain in the south of the country and the chariot was making slow progress. Just then, I noticed a young Israeli at the side of the road. I wondered, actually, whether he wanted a ride. I waved to him and he came alongside the chariot and greeted me. Then he saw the scroll of Isaiah in my hand and asked me if I understood what I was reading. I replied, "Not really. If you can help me, jump up and travel with me for a while." And that's what he did.

The young man's name was Philip. I showed him the passage I was puzzling over. It's toward the end of the scroll where Isaiah talks about someone who was suffering for the sins of someone else. I said to Philip, "Who is he talking about? Himself or someone else?"

His answer startled me. Philip replied, "He's talking about someone who was in Jerusalem quite recently. His name is Jesus."

To say I was amazed would be an understatement. Isaiah had written these words six hundred years ago. As Philip described this man Jesus and told me about his life, his public death and the way God had brought Jesus back from the dead to show people they could have their sins forgiven, I was moved to tears. Then he told me about the thousands of people in Jerusalem that had been baptised and were now followers of Jesus. I found myself drawn more and more to become a follower too.

It so happened we were approaching a watering place as he told me these things and so I said to Philip, "Will you baptise me as a new follower of Jesus?"

He paused for a few minutes and then he said, "If you truly believe in Jesus I will."

"I do believe with all my heart!" I said. And so I stopped the chariot and went down into the watering hole and he baptised me there and then. I came up out of the water overwhelmed with emotion. That remote watering hole will always have a special place in my memory because it was there that I declared my faith in Jesus in the presence of my servants.

Philip and I embraced and I travelled on to Ethiopia. I've shared my story with a number of friends now that I'm back home. There's a group of us who have now become followers of Jesus. We meet regularly to support each other in our new-found faith.

I can't help thinking though that my meeting with Philip in that isolated spot in the south of Israel wasn't a coincidence. I think God must have sent him to explain about Isaiah's "Suffering Servant", the man called Jesus.

What do you think?

(Acts 8)

An unlikely convert

My name is **Ananias** and my home is in Damascus where I belong to a group of Jewish people who have become Christians. The last few months have been quite astonishing for us and I thought you might like to hear about two wonderful miracles that happened recently.

It all began with a letter I received from a friend in Jerusalem. He was writing to tell me about the way Christians were being persecuted in his city. Apparently, one of the leaders of the Christian community, a man called Stephen, had been stoned to death for his faith and that seemed to unleash a wave of terror in the city. A young Jewish Rabbi called Saul was leading the persecution.

Perhaps I should read to you part of the letter I received:

"Rabbi Saul is a violent man. If he suspects people from the synagogue have joined the followers of Jesus, he will go to almost any lengths to attack and imprison them. Would you believe we've even had reports of home invasions by this man? None of us feel safe at the moment and the reason I am writing to you is to warn you. Rabbi Saul is now on his way to Damascus with a letter from the High Priest which gives him the power to imprison any Christians in your city."

My friend's letter left us feeling very nervous. So we started some regular meetings to pray for God's protection.

Then, about a week or two after I received the letter, I had what I can only describe as a "God Moment". It happened in the night. I was woken by a vision of the Lord Jesus. He called me by name and then He gave me the most astounding message. Jesus told me to go to Straight Street to the house of someone called Judas where I would find a man called Saul. I was to heal Saul's blindness.

Well, you can imagine my reaction. I thought it must be some sort of joke.

"Are you expecting me to help this evil man?" I replied, "The man's a maniac! He's responsible for all sorts of crimes." But before I could finish my sentence, the Lord Jesus said to me, "Ananias, just do as you are told. I know what I am doing. Saul is going to become one of my special servants to share the Good News with people everywhere." And that was it. No ifs or buts. I was simply to do what I was told.

Not surprisingly, I didn't get much sleep after that and in the morning I went round to Straight Street. It's easy to find because it is one of the main roads in Damascus. I knocked on the door and Judas showed me into the lounge.

I've got to say I was completely taken by surprise when I saw Saul. I was expecting an imposing figure, but here was a small man with thinning hair and a prominent nose. He was on his knees praying. I put my hands on his shoulders and said, "Brother Saul, receive your sight," and immediately he opened his eyes, stood up and embraced me.

We sat down to eat and Saul told me what had happened on his journey. He was travelling to Damascus with evil intent in his heart when, at about midday, he was confronted by Jesus who challenged him about the evil he was doing. The experience caused him to fall to the ground and left him blind.

Saul said to me, "Everything changed in that moment because, although the blazing light of the presence of Jesus had taken away my sight, it had illuminated my heart and mind to believe that Jesus was truly the Messiah, the Son of God, the Saviour of the world."

I would like to end this story by saying it was a peaceful end to a difficult chapter for us Christians in Damascus, but it wouldn't be wholly true.

Saul insisted on coming with me to the synagogue the next Sabbath and he started telling everyone that Jesus was the promised Messiah and they should all believe in Him. That caused many people to react strongly and, can you believe it, we ended up having to protect Saul from their anger. Rather ironic, don't you think?

Anyway, to end my story - with Saul's life in danger, the Christian community rallied round and we hid him from his new enemies. When the coast was clear, we smuggled him out of Damascus in a large basket.

Saul is back in Jerusalem now and things are quieter here. I have also heard he has changed his name to Paul.

I don't know what the Lord has got planned for me to do in the future, but I doubt if there will be a more significant task than my experience with Saul the persecutor who became Paul, an important follower of Jesus.

(Acts 9)

The good news is for everyone

My name is **Rufus** and I am a Roman soldier under the command of a centurion called Cornelius. I have served under the leadership of Cornelius for many years and I think very highly of him. He is a fine soldier and an upright man.

Recently we have been stationed in Caesarea, a coastal town in Israel. In that time Cornelius and I have actually become friends so it didn't really surprise me when he called me into his office for a chat a few weeks ago.

What did surprise me was what he asked me to do for him. He said to me, "Take two of my slaves and go down the coast to the town of Joppa and find a man called Peter. He is living in a house by the sea. Bring him back to see me."

I have to say I raised my eyebrows at his order as if to say "Pardon?" Cornelius went on to explain that in the night he had experienced a vision of an angel who had praised his good works and given Cornelius this message about Joppa. That excited me because I am a God-fearing person and I suppose it's why Cornelius selected me for the errand.

I travelled to Joppa, found the house Cornelius had mentioned, stood outside the gate and called out Peter's name. A few minutes later a tall man appeared at the gate and ushered us inside. He said, "I'm the man you are looking for and I know why you've come."

It turned out that he had also experienced a vision at that very moment. He invited us to stay the night and over supper he shared a bit of his vision with me.

Peter, or Simon Peter, to give him his full name, is a Jew but he is also a follower of Jesus. He said that because of his Jewish background he wouldn't normally eat with Gentiles because of the food we eat (Gentiles are people who aren't Jews), but God had shown him in the vision that Jesus had changed things and now he was free to eat and travel with us.

We left Joppa the next morning, accompanied by a number of Peter's friends. It's a two-day journey to Caesarea and when we arrived the next day we found Cornelius waiting for us. However, it wasn't just Cornelius but a whole crowd of his friends and relatives too – all people he had invited to his large house to hear what Peter had to share.

I will never forget what happened that day. Peter talked about his reservations regarding sharing his message with Gentiles and how God had shown him that people in any nation who fear God are acceptable to Him.

Then he told us the story of Jesus. Peter had spent about three years with Him and had come to realise He was God's Son. He told us that although Jesus had no hint of sin, he had been put to death by evil people. But God had raised Him from the dead and Jesus could now bring forgiveness to all who believe on Him.

We were all listening intently when suddenly everyone began to shout out praises to God. Then some of the crowd started to speak in other languages. God's Spirit had come amongst us to show us we were accepted into His family. It was a moving and wonderful experience, I can tell you.

I learned later that something very similar had taken place when the first Jewish people in Jerusalem

had become followers of Jesus. It was like God was confirming we Gentiles were on an equal footing with the Jews.

Actually, the people who struggled most with what happened that day were the friends Peter had brought with him. They were astounded that we Gentiles and the Jews could share the same experiences.

Peter asked Cornelius if there was somewhere he could baptise us new believers. It turned out the house we were in had a swimming pool. So all of us who believed that day were baptised immediately.

That day will be etched on my memory forever, and how it changed the relationships between Jews and Gentiles. When we get together as Christians, there's a closeness between us that wasn't there before because we have all found forgiveness through Jesus.

I think that speaks volumes, don't you?

(Acts 10)

A prayer time to remember

My name is **Rhoda** and I work for a woman called Mary who owns a big house in Jerusalem. It's quite a challenge working as a maid in a house like this because we have a lot of visitors and my job is to welcome them and look after their needs. But I enjoy working here because I am treated like family. There's a reason for this. Mary and her son, John Mark, and I are Christians and we look out for each other.

You see, there has been a lot of aggression directed at Christians in Jerusalem recently. The city's governor, King Herod, had one of our leaders killed for no other reason than the fact he was a Christian. That really distressed us, as you can imagine. His name was James and he was one of the twelve disciples of Jesus. We found ourselves worrying about who might be next. And that is what this story is about.

Because Mary has a large house it has become a place where Christians get together. Mostly we meet on Sundays because that was the day that Jesus was raised from the dead.

However, one evening recently, in the middle of the week, people began turning up at the house. It's my job to meet them at the big gates at the entrance. I thought, "That's strange, I didn't know we had a meeting tonight. I'd better get some supper organised." Then I heard the news we had all been dreading. King Herod had just arrested Simon Peter, another of our leaders.

People sat round in small groups and the atmosphere was very sad. I prepared some food but nobody had much of an appetite. Everyone felt so downcast and helpless.

After a short time, one of our elders stood up and the murmuring ceased. He said, "I know we all feel powerless at a time like this, but let's remind ourselves. Our God is more powerful than Herod and we can pray. So let's pray for Peter to be set free." So that's what we did. We got down on our knees and started praying for Peter's release.

Sometimes when we have a prayer time it's a bit sluggish with long silences, but this time it was different. We all poured out our longings to God for Peter to be set free.

I don't remember how long we had been praying, but sometime in the middle of the night I heard a knocking at the gates. I thought, "That's strange. Who on earth would be visiting us at this hour of the night?"

I went to the entrance and to my utter joy I heard the voice of Peter. I was so overcome with emotion that I left him standing outside the gate and rushed in with the news. I thought everyone would be ecstatic like I was. But they didn't believe me! Some said I had just made it up and others even suggested I'd gone mad.

While this was happening, Peter kept on knocking and eventually we all went out to open the gates and sure enough there was Peter. I felt like saying, "I told you so," but I thought that wouldn't be helpful. We brought Peter inside and he told us his story.

He had been in prison, chained to two soldiers with a couple more guarding the prison door, when an angel had appeared to him while he was sleeping. To begin with, he thought he was dreaming, but when he saw his

chains fall from his ankles, the prison door open and the guards still sleeping, he knew it was real. The angel left him in the street outside the prison wall and Peter came straight round to Mary's house.

It was a wonderful end to a prayer meeting and my friends very quickly got their appetites back! Peter left Jerusalem shortly after that before the authorities could track him down. Not long after these events, King Herod died so the crisis was over.

However, I have thought a lot, recently, about what happened that night. The thing that puzzles me is this. We were all praying for Peter to be set free, but when it happened and I said, "Peter's at the gate!" they didn't believe me. What did they expect?

Perhaps there's a lesson here for all of us? What do you expect will happen when you pray?

(Acts 12)

Not your normal prisoners

My name is **Julius** and I live in the town of Philippi. I used to serve in the Roman Army, but when I retired I became the Chief Jailer of our local prison. It's a good position, but I have to be vigilant because if a prisoner escapes the authorities hold me responsible.

Philippi is an important town because it's on one of the main roads of the Roman Empire and many people call at our town when travelling that Great East Road. The story I have to tell you concerns some travellers who called at Philippi and ended up in the town jail.

Three men had arrived from the coast. Their names were Paul, Silas and a doctor named Luke, but the story is really about the first two.

I only met Paul and Silas when they were brought to the prison, although they had been in Philippi for a number of weeks before that. They belonged to a new group called Christians and they were spreading the message about someone called Jesus.

I had heard about this man, Jesus, because other travellers passing through Philippi had mentioned him. He had lived in a remote country of the Empire called Israel, a place that is considered the last chariot stop for Romans. People talked about him doing miracles and getting offside with the Jewish authorities that eventually had him put to death. Some said there were rumours that he had risen from the tomb. I assumed these stories were exaggerated until I met Paul and Silas.

Some of the town's folk had been upset by the actions of these two men. They felt their businesses were being threatened, so they stirred up some of the citizens to cause a disturbance and it developed into a riot. Paul and Silas were brought before the magistrates.

Well, the magistrates didn't spend much time looking into who was really responsible. They took the side of the locals. Paul and Silas were severely beaten and then handed over to me to put them in my jail.

They said, "Treat these men as Category A prisoners. If they escape, you know what the consequences will be." I put them in the inner prison, chained them and secured their feet in the stocks for good measure. I thought that should keep both them and me safe. I decided to sleep at the prison that night to keep an eye on things. What I saw left me totally flabbergasted.

These two men, with their feet in the stocks and their bodies still bloodied from being beaten, started singing songs about this person Jesus and praying for the people of Philippi! I have never known any prisoners behave like that.

After a while I drifted off into a restless sleep. Sometime around midnight, I was woken by a violent earthquake, so strong that the prison doors flew open. The next few minutes are a bit of a blur. I remember thinking, "I'm done for. The prisoners will have escaped and I will be killed." So I drew my sword to kill myself. Then I heard Paul's voice from inside the prison saying, "Don't harm yourself, jailer, we are all here."

I grabbed a lantern and went into the inner prison and found Paul and Silas, free of their chains but making no attempt to escape. I was so relieved I collapsed on the floor.

Then I remembered their singing and praying and I thought, "I want what you have", so I said to them, "What do I have to do to be saved, to become a follower of Jesus?" Their reply was so simple. They said, "Just believe, that's all."

So that's what I did, right there and then. I left my staff to look after the other prisoners, and I took Paul and Silas to my office and bathed their wounds. Then I took them home to meet my family and we shared a meal together. They told us some more about Jesus and they baptised me and my family.

I think the earthquake must have unsettled the magistrates because, in the morning, they sent me this message: "Let these men go."

But Paul wasn't going quietly. He said, "I've got Roman citizenship. What they did was illegal. They can come and see us personally." That really shook the magistrates up. They came round to my house immediately to apologise and beg Paul and Silas to move on, which they agreed to do.

My family and I have now linked up with other people in our town who are also followers of Jesus.

I have mixed feelings about what happened. I think the magistrates should have got their facts straight and not acted so hastily, but if they had I might never have heard about Jesus. Life's odd sometimes, don't you think?

(Acts 16)

A meeting of minds at Mars Hill

My name is **Damaris** and I am a woman of Athens, a city that is known around the Empire for its learning and culture. My story, however, is not so much about the glory of Athens. Rather, it's about a man who visited my city and changed my way of thinking.

Let me start at the beginning. The people of Athens have always prided themselves on being open to new ideas about life and its meaning. We enjoy a good debate between people with different views and one of the venues where this happens is the market place. I like to go there to shop for my weekly supplies of groceries because there is often a public debate about the gods and religion and I'm interested in these things.

Well, a few weeks ago, I was at the market when I noticed a person I hadn't seen before in discussion with some of the regulars. Turns out that he was a visitor to Athens by the name of Paul.

I only caught snatches of the conversation, but he seemed to be talking about some new person he believed had revealed the truth. That interested me at once because I find little comfort in the vast number of shrines that are scattered around the city streets. They seem to be everywhere. I sometimes think that there are more idols in Athens than I've had Greek salads!

Later on, I heard that this visitor, Paul, had been invited to present his ideas at the public forum called the Areopagus. I thought, "That's interesting - not too many visitors are given that honour. Paul must have something to say that's worth hearing."

I should explain that the Areopagus is actually a big rock not far from the famous temple called the Acropolis on Mars Hill. A public forum is held there from time to time for our leading thinkers.

Anyway, I went along to listen. There were the usual formalities and then Paul was invited to speak. He gave an absorbing speech. I jotted down some notes of his main points. Let me share them with you:

1. The city of Athens is full of shrines to idols.
2. One shrine has the inscription "TO THE UNKNOWN GOD."
3. This is the God that Paul wanted to talk about.
4. God is not like your hand-carved idols.
5. He is closer to us than we realise.
6. He has shown us what he is really like in the person of Jesus.
7. He has confirmed the truth of this by raising Jesus from the dead after evil men had him killed.

For the most part, the audience listened to Paul, but when he started talking about Jesus being raised from the dead there was an outburst of laughter. Then some of the audience began to heckle him. Others were sceptical, but said they would like Paul to be given another opportunity to speak.

His words about the wonder of God showing Himself in Jesus struck a chord with me. It spoke into the core of my being so much that I was drawn to believe.

It was such a contrast to the sterile worship I see daily at the city's shrines. A small group of us talked to Paul for

some time after the others had departed. We also met with him several times in the few days that he remained in Athens and he explained some more about Jesus. I decided to be one of his followers.

Paul has moved on to Corinth now. He was only staying in Athens until his travelling companions, Timothy and Silas, who had been delayed in northern Greece, had caught up with him.

But the great thing is this, I now have the presence of Jesus in my life because His Spirit is with those who are believers. I get together regularly with the small group who became Christians through Paul's speech on Mars Hill. The times we share are so different from the idol worship I used to observe in Athens.

I sometimes think, "What a good thing Paul's travelling companions were delayed in Northern Greece. Otherwise I might never have come to know Jesus."

(Acts 17)

The town clerk's story

My name is **Jason** and I am the Town Clerk of the city of Ephesus. You may have heard of this city because it is famous for being the location of the Temple of Artemis, one of the Wonders of the Ancient World. We treasure our temple, both as a shrine to the ancient goddess Artemis, but also because of the visitors who come to see it. They provide a lot of income for our people.

I'm telling you this because it is part of the background to my story. It started about three years ago when a small group of people led by a man called Paul arrived in Ephesus with news of a new religion. I say "new religion", but it was really a variation of the Jewish faith. I have some Jewish friends and I learned from them that they share the same sacred writings. However, Paul and his friends believed the Messiah that God had promised in the sacred writings was someone called Jesus. He died in Jerusalem some years ago but had, they claimed, been raised from the dead.

There was a division in the local synagogue over Paul's teaching. Some Jews believed Paul's teaching, but many rejected what he was saying, so he moved into one of our learning institutions, the lecture hall of Tyranus. It made sense really because, as Paul said, "God sent His Son Jesus to show what He was like, not just to the Jewish people, but to the whole world."

It was in the lecture hall that I first heard Paul speak. For about two years he gave lectures about this new faith and many of the Ephesian citizens went along to hear him. Quite a few became Christians or followers of "The Way" as people called them.

I didn't become a Christian, but I couldn't help being impressed with what was happening. God was obviously blessing people through Paul and through the name of Jesus. I heard reports of people being healed of all sorts of diseases. Would you believe some even claimed they were healed when touched by Paul's clothing?

His preaching was having a big effect on some people's behaviour. We have a lot of witchcraft in our city and many people who practised witchcraft also became Christians. To show they had finished with their past activities, they got all their witchcraft books together and made a public bonfire. It was a spectacular sight.

The truth of the matter is that Paul's preaching was having a positive impact on Ephesus and, as the Town Clerk, that pleased me.

But then everything changed. It happened this way. A group of people in Ephesus, who made a lot of money by selling miniature silver replicas of the temple to visitors, began to feel threatened by Paul's teaching against idolatry. So they started spreading rumours to turn people against him. The stories weren't true, but once the rumour mill got going there was no holding it back.

A massive crowd formed and they rushed into the temple. There were thousands of people all shouting and yelling. The leader of the group of silversmiths was a man called Demetrius and he worked the crowd into a rage against Paul. For two hours they shouted, "Great is Artemis of the Ephesians."

Paul wanted to go in and speak to the crowd to try and calm them down but some of our leading citizens who

respected Paul managed to talk him out of it. It was just as well. I think Paul might well have been killed.

Eventually I managed to quieten the crowd, although I think they were so hoarse they had no voice left. I said to them, "Everyone knows about the great Artemis and her famous temple. Paul and his friends have not broken any laws. They are good people and if Demetrius has a problem with them he should take it to the courts."

I scolded them for being involved in the riot. I said, "Today's disturbance may be reported to the Emperor in Rome and there might be consequences." Finally, I ordered them to go home.

Thankfully that was the end of the crisis. Paul and his friends moved on soon after the riot, but they have left behind many new Christians who are fine citizens.

These recent events have made me think. I'm pleased to have this Christian presence in our city because these people are a force for good. But the Christian faith seems to cause quite a reaction with some people. I sometimes wonder if what we are seeing is the clash of two kingdoms, one of Light and one of Darkness. What do you think about what happened?

(Acts 19)

Trouble in Jerusalem

My name is **Bartholomew**, but my friends call me Bart. I live in Jerusalem and it's an exciting city to live in. Jerusalem is the place where our big Jewish Temple stands so we get thousands of visitors coming to worship there. But sometimes it can get a bit scary because the Roman governor lives here. There are always a lot of soldiers around.

The story I am about to tell you actually begins in the Temple. It sends a shiver down my spine even now when I think about what I got involved in.

Let me start at the beginning. My mother is called Rachel and she has a brother who has become quite famous. Years ago he lived in Jerusalem and people knew him as Saul, the Rabbi who hated Christians. Something happened to him and he became one of the leading Christians and he changed his name to Paul. This brought him enemies, but he didn't care. He went everywhere telling people that Jesus was God's special person. That made some people even angrier and that's the background to this story.

When I say Uncle Paul went everywhere, I mean everywhere. He travelled all over the Roman world to places I'd never heard of. Wherever he went, people became followers of Jesus. We used to get letters from time to time about where my uncle was and what was happening to him and his travelling companion, Silas. I used to love reading about their adventures.

Well, a few weeks ago Uncle Paul arrived back in Jerusalem. It was so exciting to see him again. We had a special meal to welcome him home.

A few days later, he went off to the Temple and that's when the drama began.

Some of the Jews who remembered my uncle, and had never forgiven him for becoming a Christian, recognised him and started to accuse him of things he hadn't done. Next thing, a crowd had formed and things got really ugly. If it hadn't been for the Roman soldiers sent to sort out the problem, I think my uncle might have been killed on the spot.

The soldiers assumed Uncle Paul must have done something wrong so they arrested him and took him into their custody, partly for his own protection and partly to find out what he had done.

The Tribune - that's the commander of the soldiers - told his men to tie Paul up and whip him to find out what he had done to cause such uproar. The Tribune got the shock of his life when my uncle told him he was breaking the law by tying him up. He didn't realise that my uncle had Roman citizenship and he might get into big trouble.

This is where I come into the story. I was in one of the eating-houses in Jerusalem when I overheard a group of men sitting around one of the tables talking. I heard words like "hate him", "troublemaker", and "get rid of him". It was then it dawned on me that they were talking about my uncle. So I really listened hard and what I heard shocked me. Apparently 40 men had taken an oath that they wouldn't eat or drink anything until they had killed Uncle Paul.

The plan was for the priests to ask the commander to bring Paul to the High Priest and these 40 men would ambush him on the way and kill him.

I decided I needed to act quickly. I didn't tell my mother because she would probably worry. Instead, I went to the Roman barracks and, because my uncle is a Roman citizen and has some privileges, I was allowed to talk to him alone.

Uncle Paul listened and then he told the soldier who was on guard duty to take me to the commander. So I told my story all over again. The commander said to me, "Don't breathe a word of this to anyone." Then I was ushered out of the barracks. That night the commander ordered 200 of his soldiers to escort Paul to another city where he would be safe.

I never saw my Uncle Paul again after that. Eventually they took him all the way to Rome.

Sometimes I wonder what might have happened if I hadn't acted on what I heard. I also wonder about the 40 men who vowed not to eat anything until they killed Paul. They must be pretty hungry by now, don't you think?

I'm just pleased that I had a part to play in saving my uncle so that he could go on telling people about Jesus. It's a good reminder that God uses young people too.

(Acts 24)

Two Governors, a King and Paul

Hi. It's **Bart** here again. Last time, I told you about how my Uncle Paul was arrested and how God used me to save him from being killed. There was a plot to ambush my uncle in Jerusalem, but he was safely transferred to another city.

Well, that was the last time I saw my uncle, but it was by no means the end of the story.

Paul is a good letter writer and we got a number of letters from him telling us about his experiences in the new city of Caesarea. My mum kept his letters and they make an amazing story. I thought you might like to hear what happened.

A few days after Paul arrived in Caesarea, the people who wanted him dead went from Jerusalem to see the Roman governor of that city. They tried to get him to do away with my uncle, but the governor, whose name was Felix, told them he would deal with the matter in his own time and so my uncle's enemies had to return to Jerusalem empty-handed.

Felix was actually quite interested to know about the Christian faith and for the next two years he got Paul to come and talk to him about Jesus. He was also hoping Paul's friends would quietly slip him some money so he would set my uncle free. But it didn't happen and Felix was transferred to another part of the Roman Empire while Paul stayed in prison.

The new governor was a man called Festus. He had only been there a few weeks when my uncle's enemies saw their chance to get rid of him for good. They went up to Caesarea and asked Festus to send Paul back to Jerusalem to be put on trial. They planned to ambush Paul's party on the way up to Jerusalem just like they had planned to do previously.

But Uncle Paul is not stupid. He guessed what they were up to. So when Festus asked him if he was willing to go to Jerusalem to answer his accusers, Paul replied, "I am a Roman citizen and therefore I have the right to be tried before the Emperor. I now claim that right." That really shut Paul's enemies up, but it left Governor Festus scratching his head. He had to send my uncle to Rome to stand trial before the Emperor, but he couldn't understand why Paul was in prison in the first place. He didn't seem to have done anything wrong. It all seemed to centre on a difference of opinion about someone called Jesus.

Then an interesting thing happened. King Agrippa, who knew a lot about the Jewish religion because his wife, Bernice, was a Jew, decided to visit Caesarea. So Festus arranged for my Uncle Paul to explain to Festus, the King and Queen and other VIPs why he was a prisoner.

I wish I could have been there. My uncle's letters said that he told them the story of his life: how he grew up as a strict Jewish Pharisee; how he hated the Jews who believed Jesus was the "Promised One"; how he got them put in prison and even had them killed; how, when his anger towards Christians was at its height, Jesus met him and challenged him to be his follower; and how he was blinded for three days before a Christian called Ananias prayed for him to get his sight back. Then Paul told them about his wish to tell people everywhere about Jesus who was God's Son, who died and was raised from the dead so people could have their sins forgiven.

When he had finished, Governor Festus called out, "Paul, you've read too many books and this has made you insane." My uncle said, "I'm not mad", and then turned to the King and said, "King Agrippa, you believe the prophets. I know you do. They all spoke about the coming of Jesus and you will have heard the story of Jesus because it is public knowledge. It didn't happen in secret."

That put the King on the spot. He didn't know how to reply, so he said, "Do you think you have persuaded me to be a Christian, Paul?" To which my uncle replied, "I wish that you and everyone here today could become a Christian like I am. But I don't wish these chains on you."

Then the meeting finished and Paul was taken back to his prison cell to wait for a ship to take him to Rome. I'm so proud of my uncle. He was prepared to tell the truth about following Jesus even though it cost him his freedom. It makes me think about my responsibility to do the same.

(Acts 25 & 26)

Paul's dangerous voyage to Rome

My name is **Luke**. You may have heard of me because I wrote one of the stories of the life of Jesus. I am a doctor and I travel a lot. I want to tell you about the most amazing journey I have ever experienced.

I am a close friend of Paul, the Christian leader, and when I was in Jerusalem recently I visited his sister to find out how he was getting on. She said, "Haven't you heard? He's in prison in Caesarea," and then she told me the story of how it had happened. I decided to go to Caesarea to see my old friend, but when I arrived I found Paul with a whole lot of other prisoners about to be put on a ship to Rome.

I had a quick chat to the captain and he agreed to sell me a ticket and so we set off on the Mediterranean. I was able to see quite a lot of my friend because the centurion in charge of the prisoners had taken a liking to him. I think he realised Paul was very different from the other prisoners in his care who looked to be a bunch of pretty hardened criminals. We stopped at the coastal city of Sidon to take on supplies, then we went close to the island of Cyprus and landed in a port called Myra. We had to change ships there to get to Rome and then we set sail again, but progress was quite slow because there wasn't a lot of wind. Eventually, we sailed into a port on the island of Crete called Fair Havens.

Fair Havens wasn't fair at all. It was a real one-horse town with nothing for the sailors to do and because winter was approaching it was becoming quite dangerous for sailing. Paul told the centurion that we needed to spend the winter there, but the ship's captain said, "I don't want to stay in this dump of a town," and so, against my friend Paul's advice, we set sail.

The first couple of days were okay with a tail wind, but then everything changed. We sailed right into a hurricane. It's called the Nor'easter and is every sailor's nightmare - lots of ships have been sunk by this wind in the past.

The next two weeks were the most scary I have ever experienced. The storm raged on, day and night, and the sailors lost control of the ship. The waves kept swamping the decks, we hardly ate anything and sleep was out of the question.

The captain ordered the crew to throw the cargo overboard to make the ship lighter, but it didn't make much difference. So they planned to throw the ship's anchors into the sea to slow the ship down if we got near land. Anyway, after two weeks of this, an amazing thing happened. Paul - and don't forget he was one of the prisoners - got everyone together when there was a lull in the storm and talked to the crew.

First he said, "I told you we shouldn't sail, but you wouldn't listen." Then he said, "Last night an angel of my God stood by me and told me, "Don't be afraid. You will all be safe. No one on board is going to die, but the ship is doomed. Now let us have something to eat to give us some strength." Then he thanked God and we had a meal. It wasn't long after that we sighted land. The soldiers said to Julius the centurion, "Let's kill the prisoners because they might escape", but because he wanted to protect Paul, Julius said, "No."

Somehow, we all got to the shore safely, the ship broke up and sank and all 279 of us huddled together on the beach.

But that wasn't the end of the story. We had landed on the island of Malta. We made a fire to keep warm and Paul was putting some wood on the fire when a poisonous snake bit him. He shook it off into the fire and everyone thought he would die, but when nothing happened to him they thought Paul must be a god.

Anyway, we saw lots of wonderful things happen in the months we spent on Malta. The local people were so kind to us and while we were there people who were sick came to Paul to be prayed for and he also told them about Jesus.

Eventually another ship called at the island and we sailed for Italy and Rome. But they didn't put Paul in prison while he waited for his trial. They let him live in his own house with a guard to keep an eye on him and he was allowed to have his friends come and visit. And that's where I left my friend.

(Acts 27 & 28)

The man who nearly died

My name is **Epaphroditus**, but people call me Paffi. I live in the city of Philippi. My father was a Roman soldier and when he retired from the army he was given a house in Philippi.

I want to tell you some things that have happened in Philippi in the last few years, things that have changed my life completely.

As I said, our family are Romans and we used to worship Roman gods when I was growing up, but when I became old enough to think for myself, I began to find out about other religions.

One day, a couple of Jewish preachers, named Paul and Silas, came to Philippi. They started to tell people there was only one God and he had sent his son Jesus to show the world how he loved everyone. Apparently, Jesus lived in a far away country called Israel and the Roman governor there had him put to death. But God raised Jesus to life again.

Well, there was a lot of trouble in the town after people heard what Paul and Silas said. They were beaten and put in jail for causing trouble. Then there was an earthquake while they were in prison. So they were asked to leave the town.

After they had gone, some of us who believed the story of Jesus started getting together each Sunday in the home of a businesswoman called Lydia. We became a small church with several nationalities and we all try to help each other to be true followers of Jesus.

This all happened several years ago. Since then, Paul has visited us several times. However, about six months ago we got some sad news. We heard that Paul had been arrested and taken to Rome where he was in prison awaiting a trial before the Roman Emperor.

When we heard the news, we all got together to pray for our friend and while we were praying someone said, "Why don't we all contribute to a gift parcel for Paul. One of us could travel to Rome to take the gift to Paul and then he will know that we are praying for him and thinking about him."

Everyone was in agreement and then someone said, "Paffi's not married, he could be our courier." I was thrilled at the suggestion and a bit scared too because there are bandits that will rob you on the journey to Rome. There is a good road, the Great East Road, which goes through Philippi all the way to the coast. So I went that way, keeping close to other travellers where I could.

When I arrived in Rome it took a few days to find where Paul was imprisoned. When we met, he was so thrilled to see me and to hear about our church and all the members. Paul and I didn't have much privacy because there were always two Roman soldiers with him.

I stayed in Rome for a few weeks, visiting Paul most days, but then something happened - I caught a fever. At first, it didn't seem too bad, but then I felt really terrible, coughing up blood and struggling to breathe. I don't remember what happened after that because I went into a coma. Some Christians in the church at Rome lovingly cared for me until I eventually woke up. They told me that I had nearly died.

Gradually I started to get better. When I was well enough I went to see Paul to tell him I was going to return to Philippi. He wept when he saw me because he

had been praying that my life would be spared. Then Paul handed me a big envelope. He said, "I've written a letter to all you Christians at Philippi and I want you to take it with you when you leave Rome."

I shall never forget the last time I visited Paul. He said good-bye, saying that he was torn in two directions. He would like to come with me, but he was also looking forward to being with Jesus if the trial judge condemned him to die. Anyway, he hugged me so tight when I said good-bye.

I'm back in Philippi now. We've read the letter in church several times. Some of it's personal and other parts explain a bit more about why Jesus came and what His death means to us. We treasure that letter. Paul mentions me and my sickness and how I nearly died. I hope you get the chance to read the letter (it's called Philippians) some day.

(Philippians 2 v 25-30)

A very special letter

My name is **Timothy**. I grew up in a town called Lystra with my parents and grandparents. My mother's name is Eunice and my grandmother is Lois. My story begins in Lystra although it is a long time since I lived there. My father was a Greek, but my mother was a Jew and her parents were Jews too. So when I was young I learned about the books of Moses and the ancient prophets.

One day two men came to our town – their names were Paul and Barnabas, and they came to our synagogue and told us about a person called Jesus who they said was God's promised Messiah. My mother and grandmother became believers in Jesus, but I wasn't too sure to start with.

Anyway, we had a man in our town who had never walked. When Paul saw him, he said, "In the name of Jesus, get up and walk," and the man walked. And I became a believer in Jesus.

In the beginning, everyone was excited. They thought Paul and Barnabas were gods. But then things turned nasty and a mob of people stoned Paul to death – at least that's what they thought they had done. But after they dragged his body out of the city, he got up and walked away.

I suppose it was about two years after this that Paul returned to our town with another friend called Silas. By this time, we had formed a small church in our house for people who had become Christians and Paul and Silas stayed with us.

When it was time for them to move on to the next town, they invited me to go with them. My grandmother wasn't too keen, but she didn't stop me and my great adventure began. It would take me days to tell you all the things that happened over the next few years.

We visited some famous towns and cities. We saw miracles happen. Many people became believers in Jesus. Sometimes we were attacked by angry people and put in prison.

Eventually I settled in a city called Ephesus to help the local Christians. Paul left me there and carried on with his job of taking the story of Jesus to new places.

I didn't hear from Paul for quite a while, although I prayed every day that God would look after him. There were stories that he had been arrested and taken to a prison in Rome.

Then one day there was a knock on the door and when I opened the door, there, standing in front of me was someone with a letter from the man who had introduced me to Jesus.

Paul had written to me once before to explain some of the things about following Jesus that I needed to know so I could tell others. But this letter made me both happy and sad - happy because my friend Paul was still praying for me, and sad because he was in prison. He was not only feeling the cold of the winter in Rome, but was also expecting to be put to death because he refused to stop telling people about Jesus.

I have treasured these letters from Paul. People have asked me if they can borrow them, but I always refuse to let them out of my sight. But I have let some people copy them so that others can read them.

www.ingramcontent.com/pod-product-compliance
Lightning Source LLC
Chambersburg PA
CBHW041157290426
44108CB00003B/94